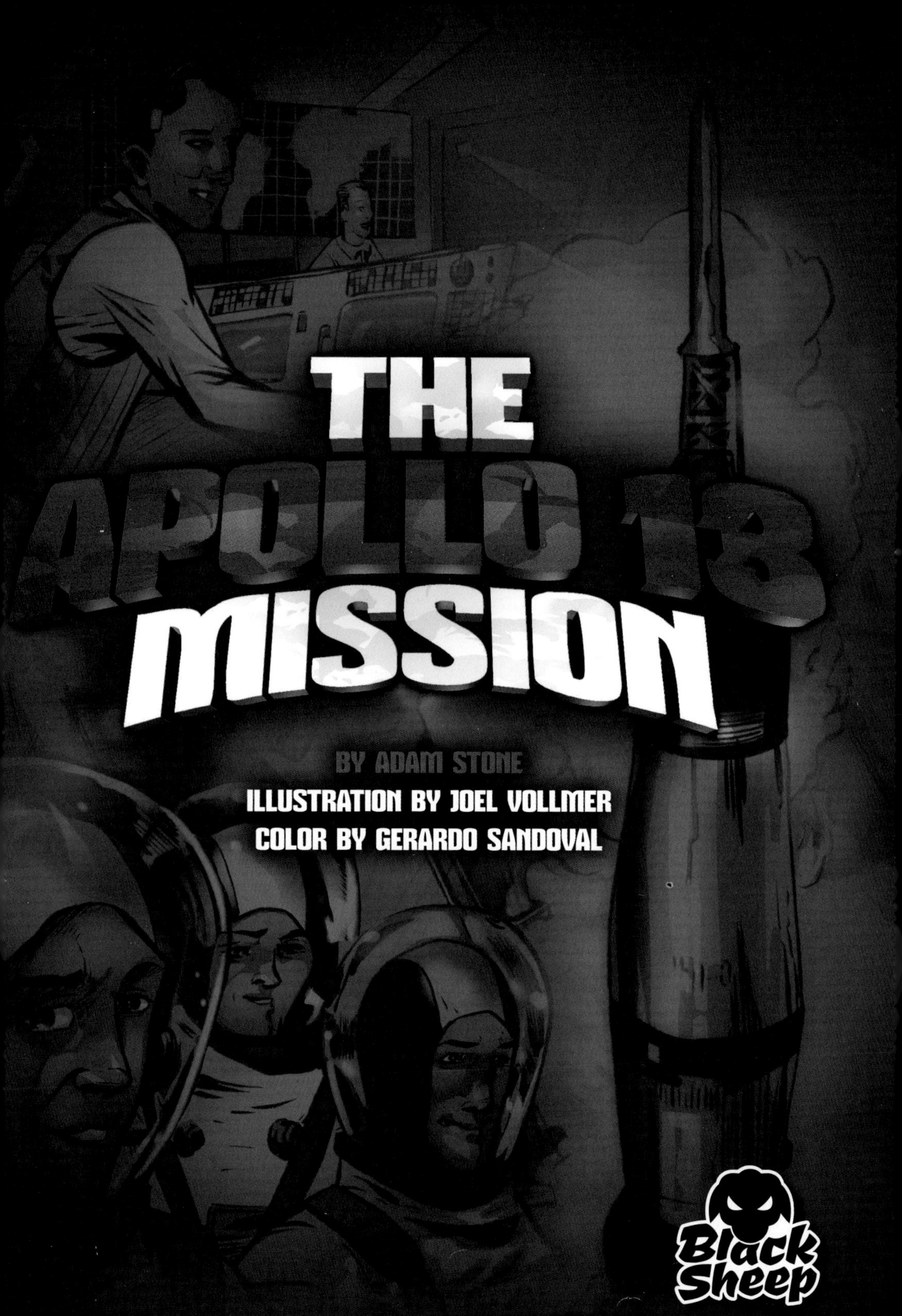

THE APOLLO 13 MISSION

BY ADAM STONE
ILLUSTRATION BY JOEL VOLLMER
COLOR BY GERARDO SANDOVAL

Black Sheep

BELLWETHER MEDIA • MINNEAPOLIS, MN

STRAY FROM REGULAR READS WITH BLACK SHEEP BOOKS. FEEL A RUSH WITH EVERY READ!

Library of Congress Cataloging-in-Publication Data

Stone, Adam, author.
The Apollo 13 Mission / by Adam Stone.
pages cm. -- (Black Sheep. Disaster Stories)
Includes bibliographical references and index.
Summary: "Exciting illustrations follow the events of the Apollo 13 mission. The combination of brightly colored panels and leveled text is intended for students in grades 3 through 7"-- Provided by publisher.
ISBN 978-1-62617-149-7 (hardcover : alk. paper)
1. Apollo 13 (Spacecraft)--Juvenile literature. 2. Apollo 13 (Spacecraft)--Comic books, strips, etc. 3. Project Apollo (U.S.)--Juvenile literature. 4. Project Apollo (U.S.)--Comic books, strips, etc. 5. Space vehicle accidents--Juvenile literature. 6. Space vehicle accidents--Comic books, strips, etc. I. Title. II. Title: Apollo Thirteen mission.
TL789.8.U6S76 2014
629.45'4--dc23
2014012560

This edition first published in 2015 by Bellwether Media, Inc.

Printed in the United States of America, North Mankato, MN.

Table of Contents

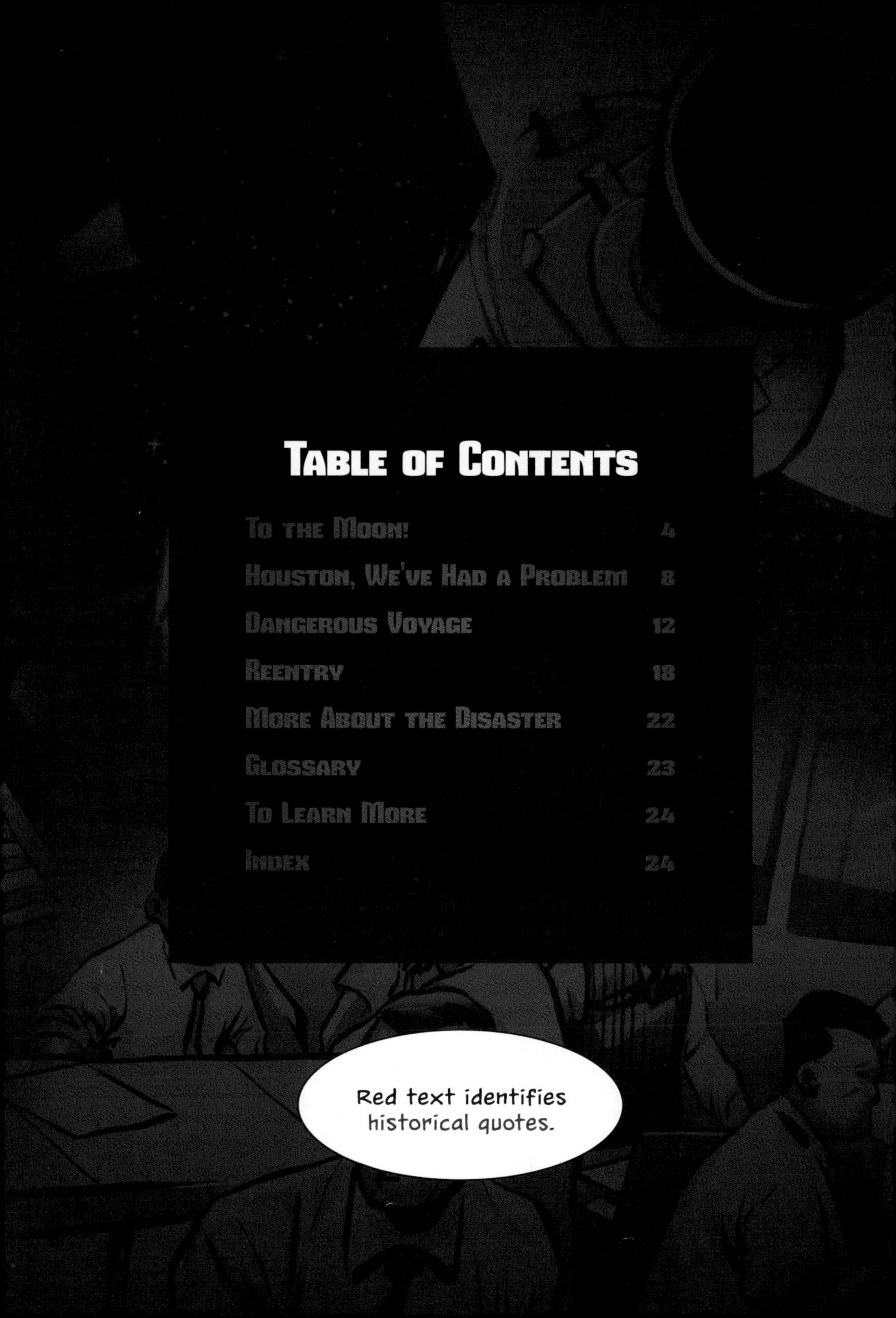

Red text identifies historical quotes.

To the Moon!

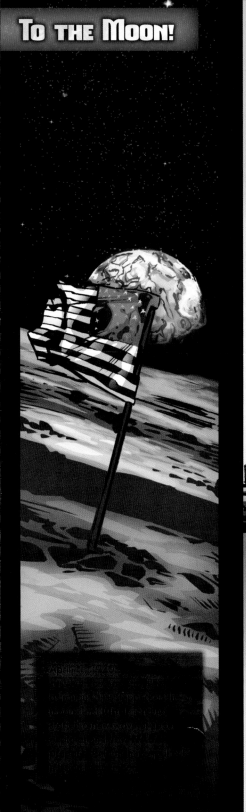

Commander James Lovell, **command module** pilot Jack Swigert, and **lunar module** pilot Fred Haise have trained for this mission for years. The original pilot, Ken Mattingly, was pulled three days before due to exposure to the measles.

I'm so excited to be part of this trip. I couldn't believe it when I got the call.

It's quite the lucky break for you, Jack.

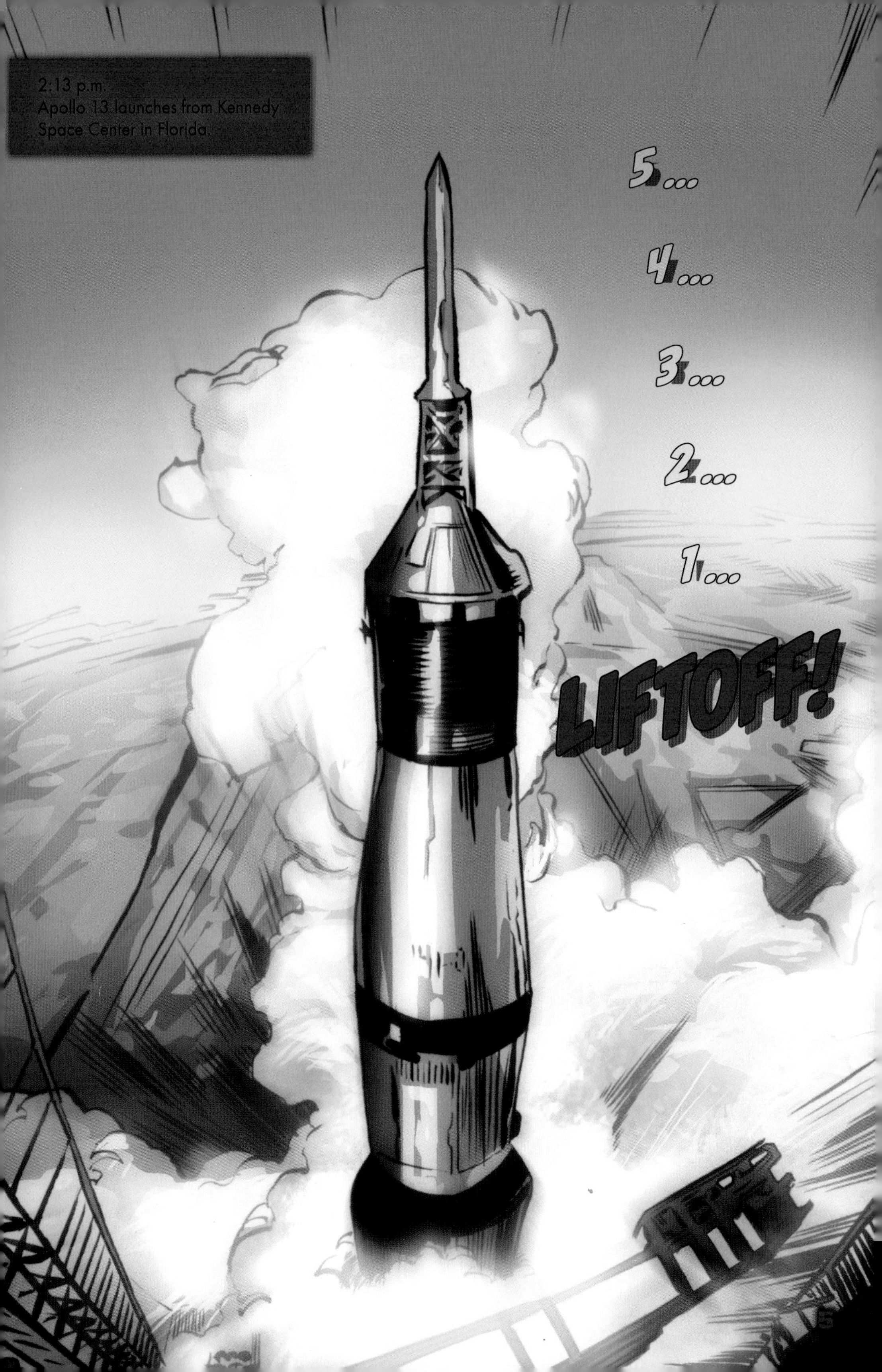
2:13 p.m.
Apollo 13 launches from Kennedy Space Center in Florida.
5...
4...
3...
2...
1...
LIFTOFF!

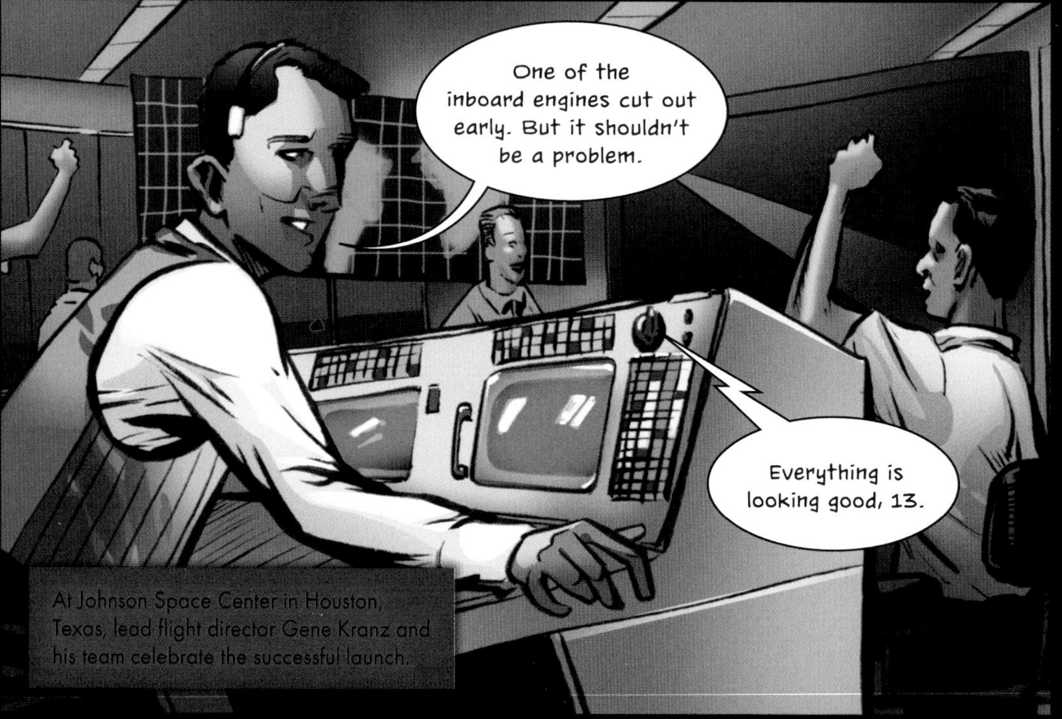
One of the inboard engines cut out early. But it shouldn't be a problem.
Everything is looking good, 13.
At Johnson Space Center in Houston, Texas, lead flight director Gene Kranz and his team celebrate the successful launch.

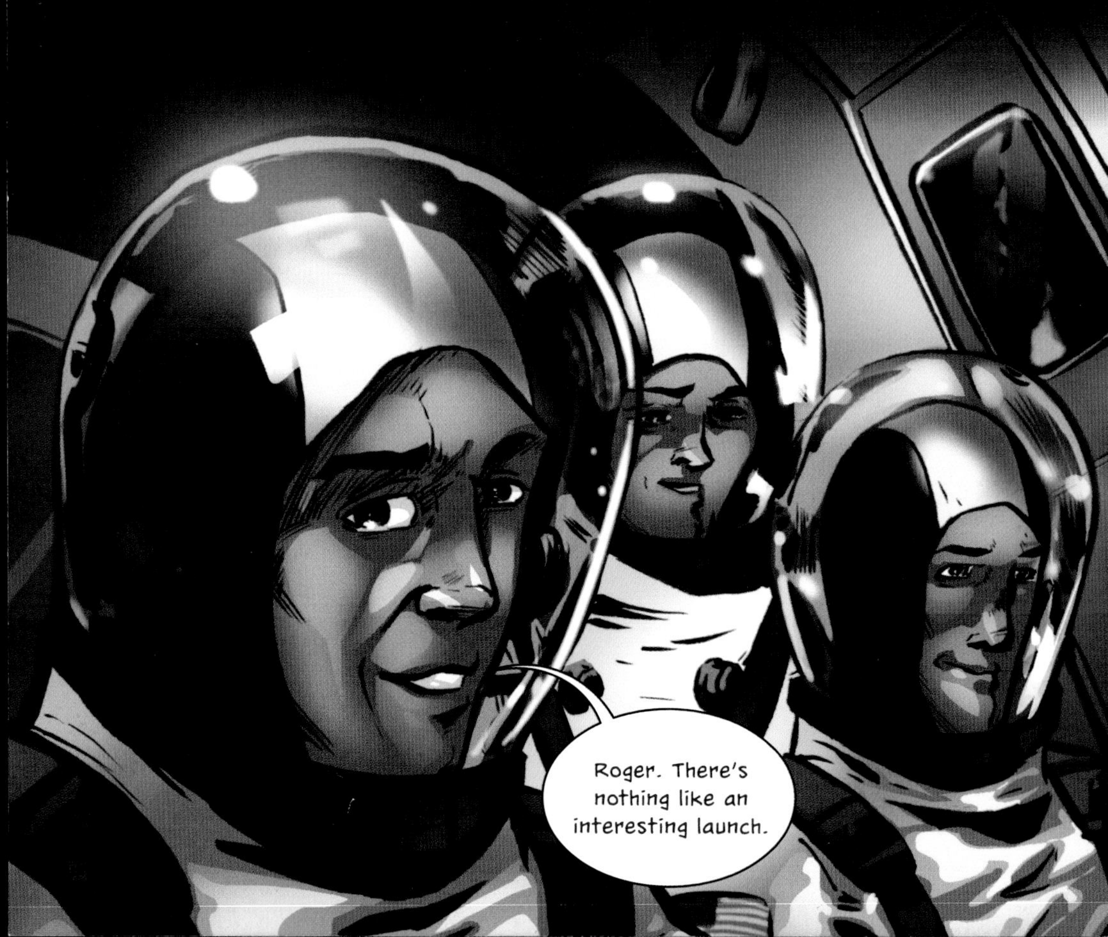
Roger. There's nothing like an interesting launch.

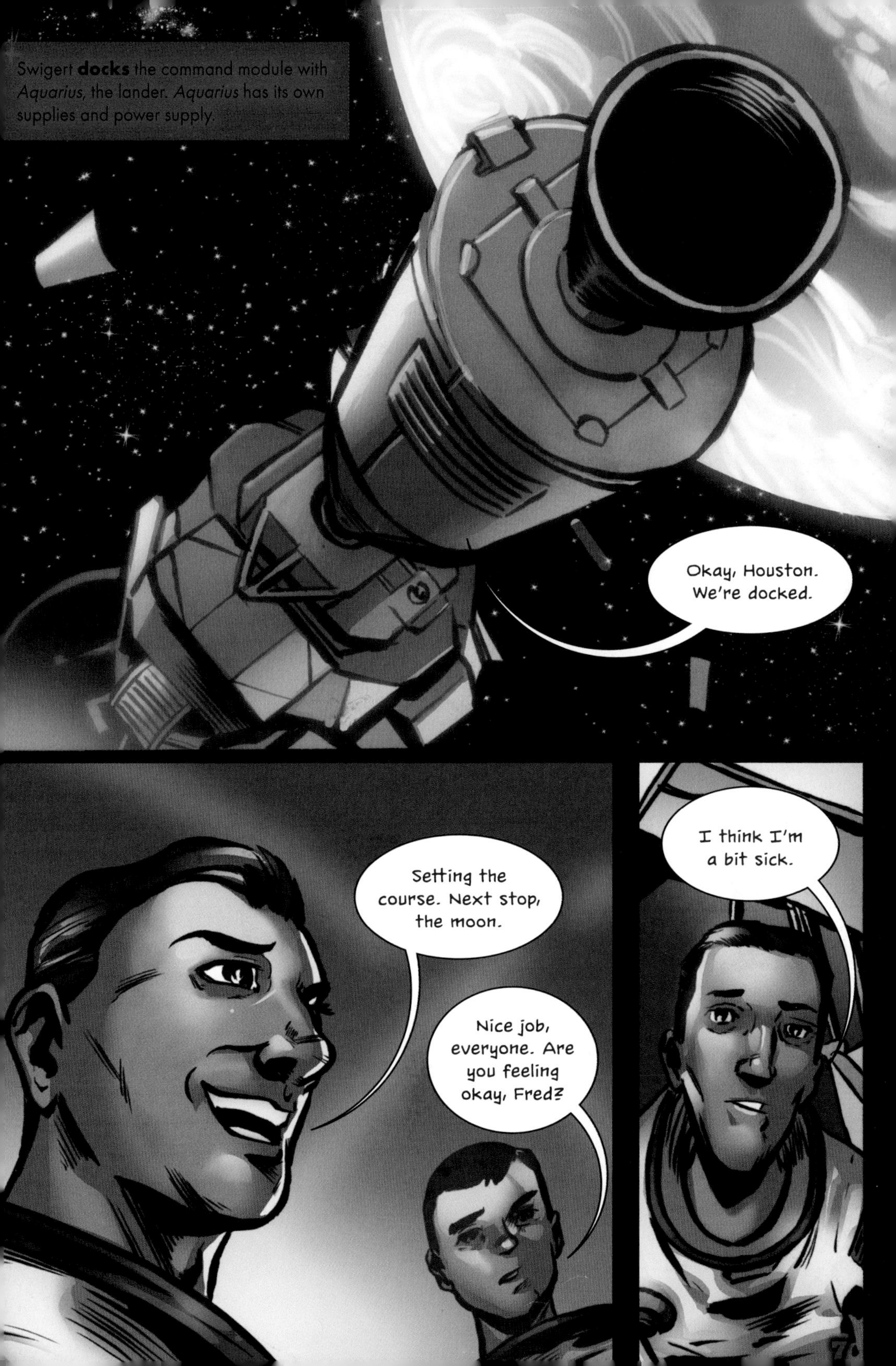
Swigert **docks** the command module with *Aquarius*, the lander. *Aquarius* has its own supplies and power supply.
Okay, Houston. We're docked.
Setting the course. Next stop, the moon.
Nice job, everyone. Are you feeling okay, Fred?
I think I'm a bit sick.

Houston, We've Had a Problem

April 13, 1970, 56 hours after launch: The astronauts are about a day away from the moon. **Mission Control** asks Swigert to turn the oxygen tank fans on in the **service module**. This is a normal procedure.

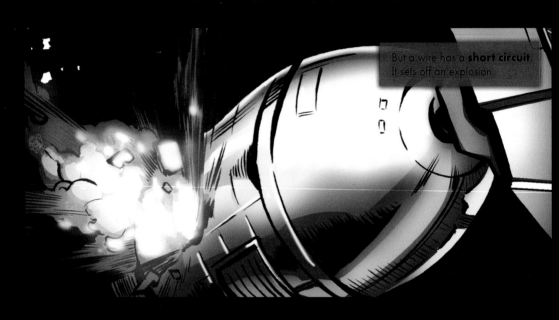

But a wire has a **short circuit**. It sets off an explosion.

What was that?

The oxygen pressure is dropping. So is our power.

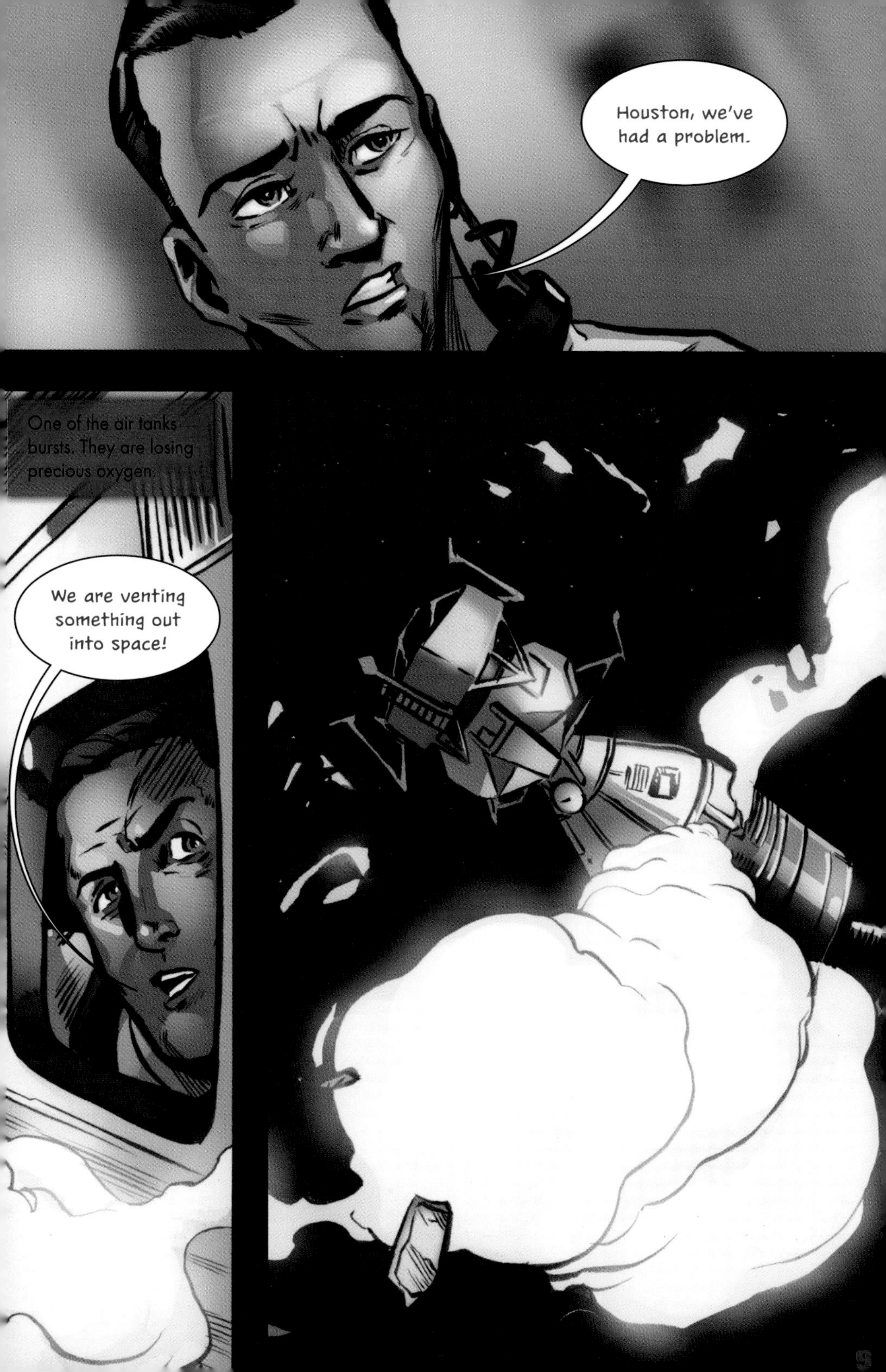
Houston, we've had a problem.
One of the air tanks bursts. They are losing precious oxygen.
We are venting something out into space!

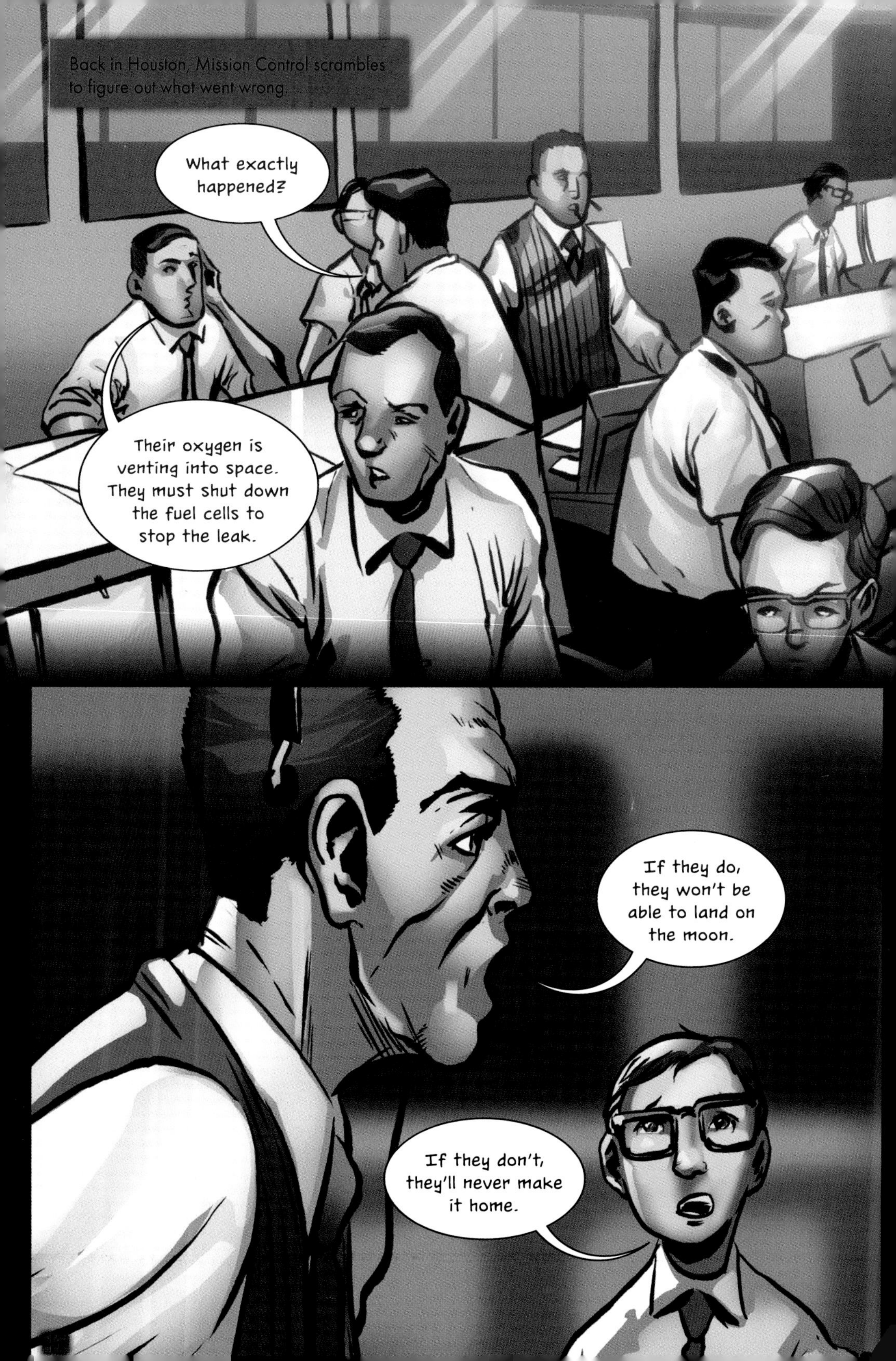
Back in Houston, Mission Control scrambles to figure out what went wrong.
What exactly happened?
Their oxygen is venting into space. They must shut down the fuel cells to stop the leak.
If they do, they won't be able to land on the moon.
If they don't, they'll never make it home.

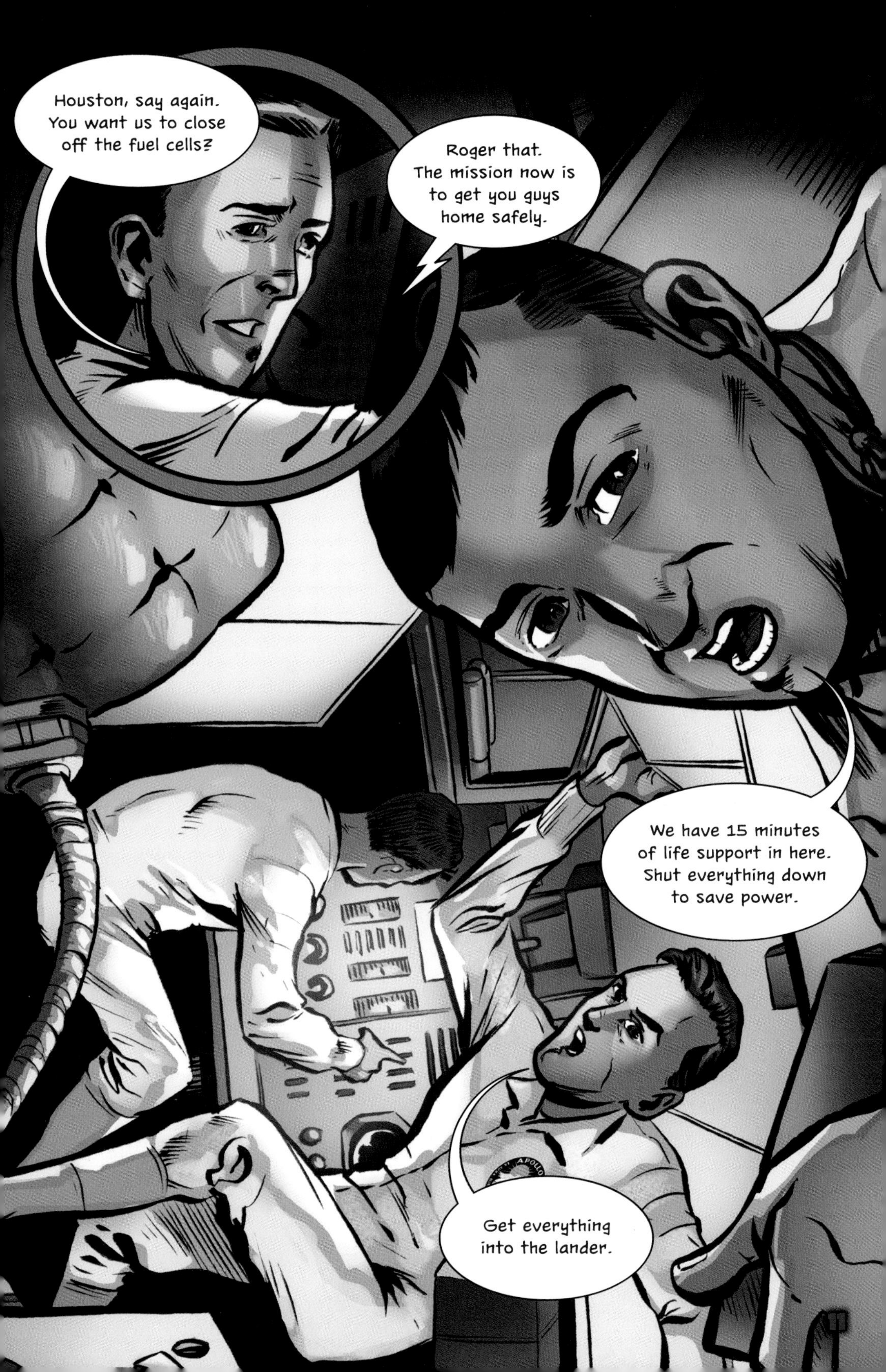
Houston, say again. You want us to close off the fuel cells?
Roger that. The mission now is to get you guys home safely.
We have 15 minutes of life support in here. Shut everything down to save power.
Get everything into the lander.

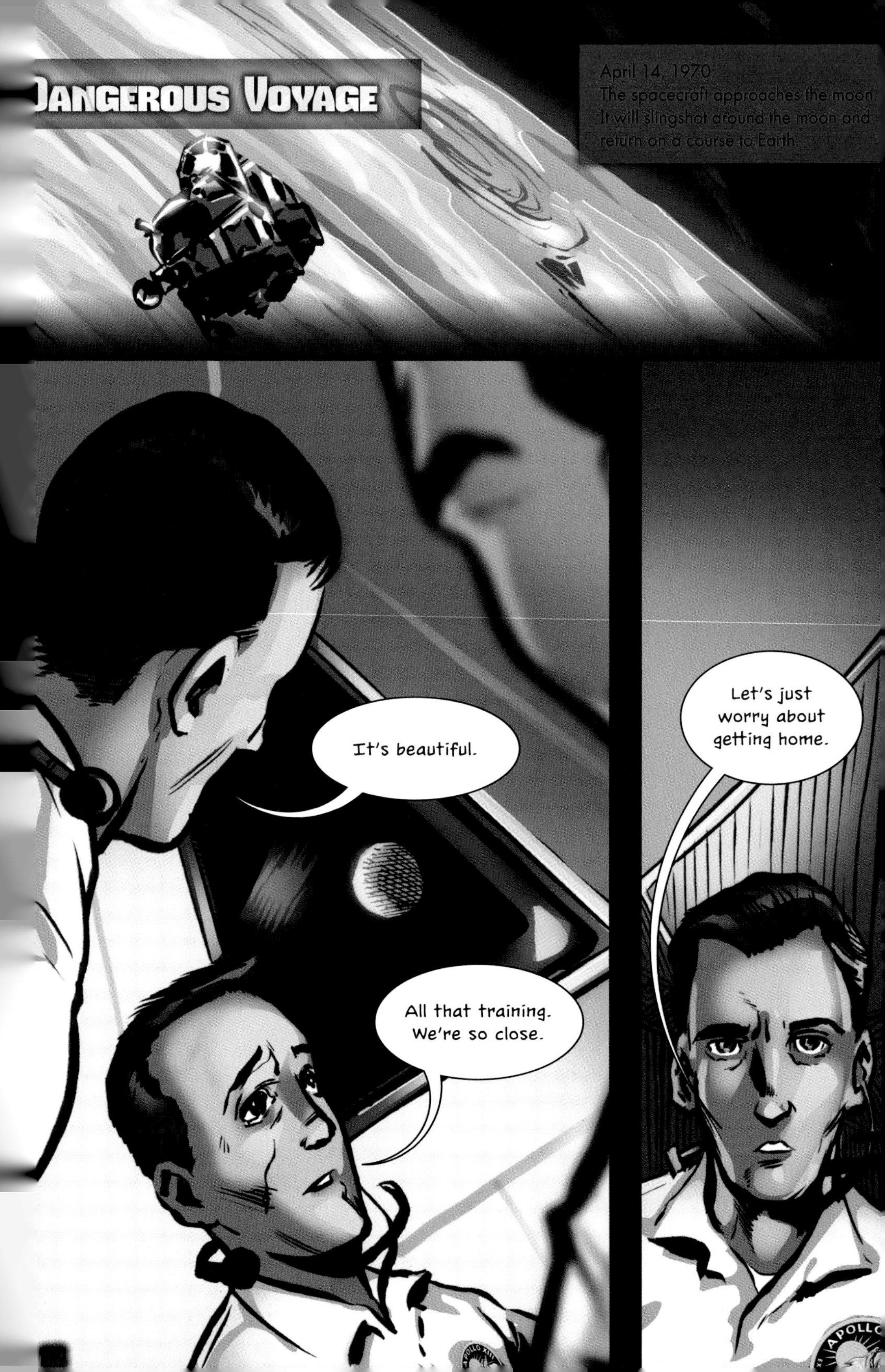
Dangerous Voyage
April 14, 1970:
The spacecraft approaches the moon. It will slingshot around the moon and return on a course to Earth.
It's beautiful.
All that training. We're so close.
Let's just worry about getting home.

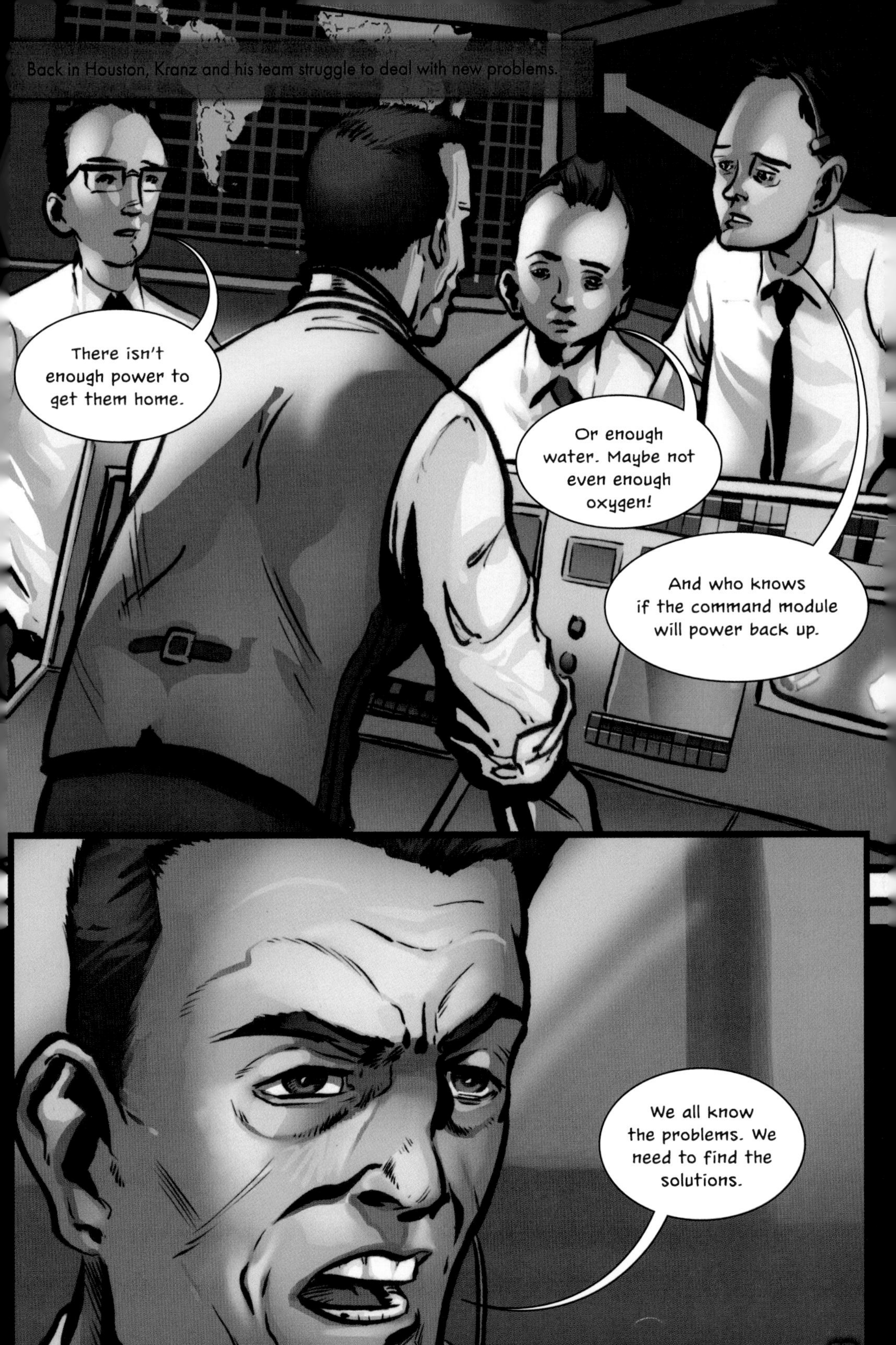
Back in Houston, Kranz and his team struggle to deal with new problems.
There isn't enough power to get them home.
Or enough water. Maybe not even enough oxygen!
And who knows if the command module will power back up.
We all know the problems. We need to find the solutions.

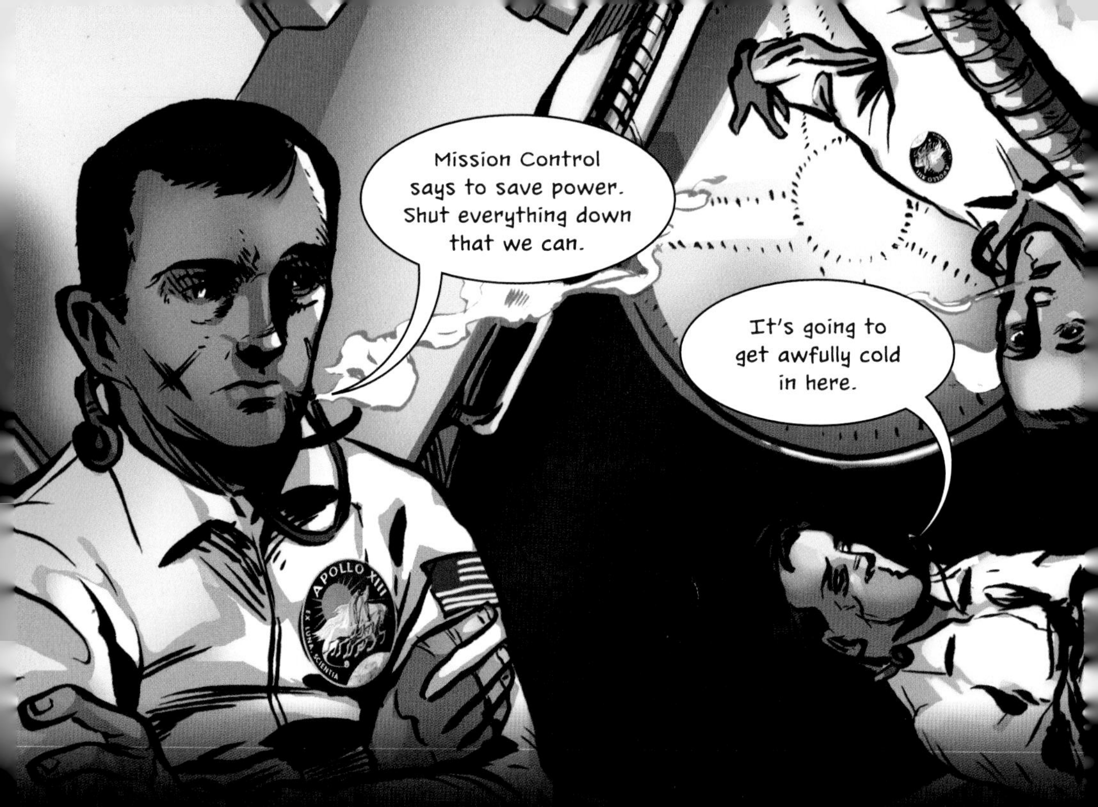
Mission Control says to save power. Shut everything down that we can.
It's going to get awfully cold in here.

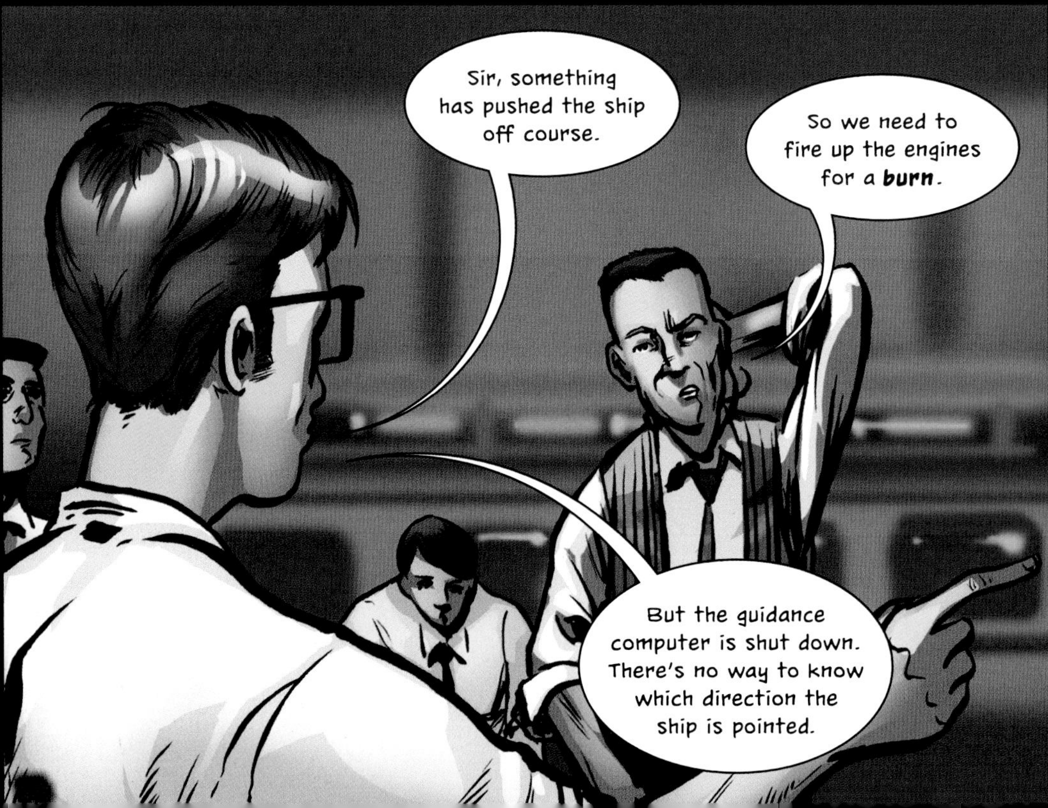
Sir, something has pushed the ship off course.
So we need to fire up the engines for a **burn**.
But the guidance computer is shut down. There's no way to know which direction the ship is pointed.

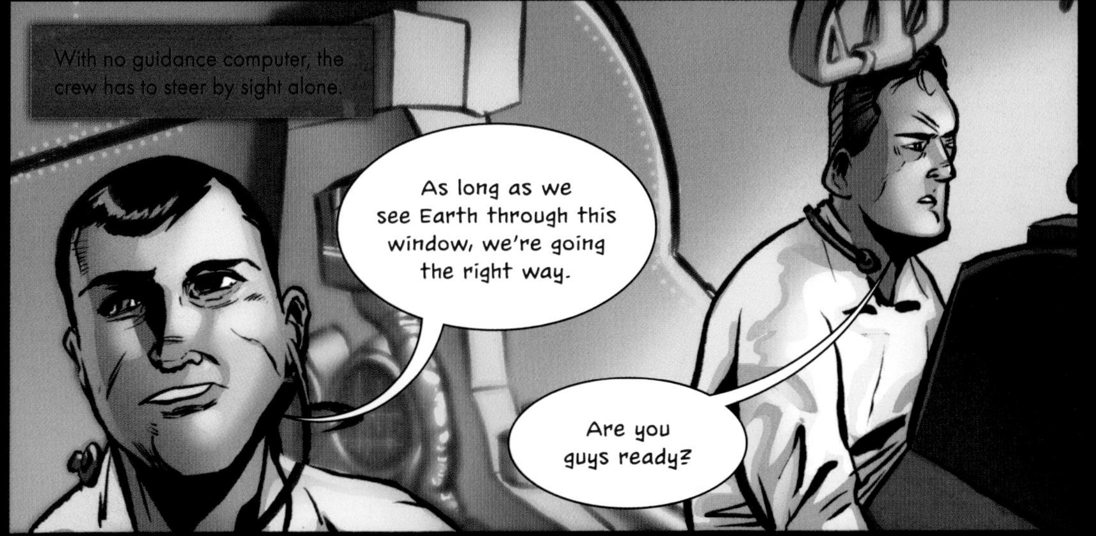
With no guidance computer, the crew has to steer by sight alone.
As long as we see Earth through this window, we're going the right way.
Are you guys ready?

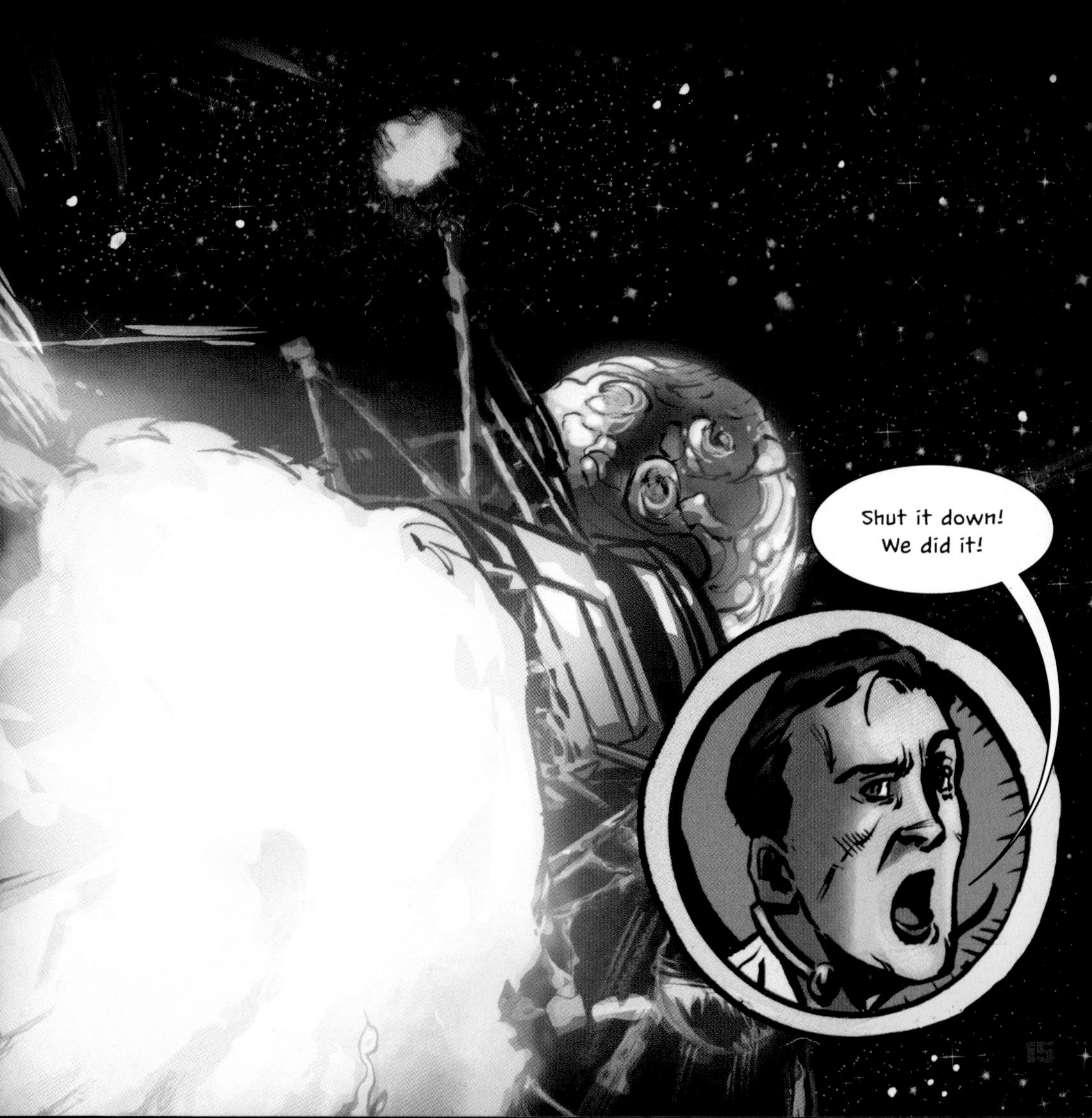
Shut it down! We did it!

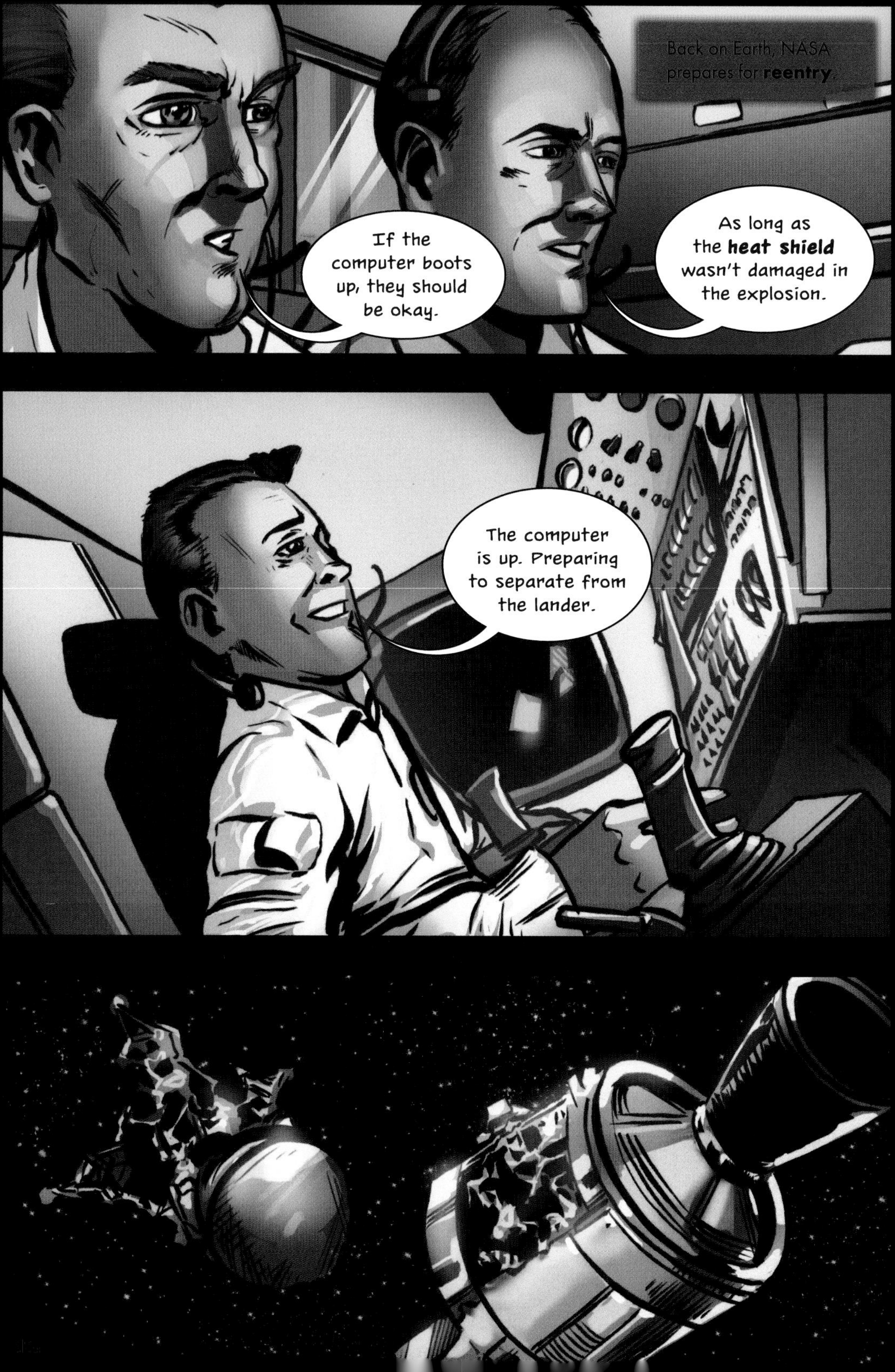
Back on Earth, NASA prepares for **reentry**.
If the computer boots up, they should be okay.
As long as the **heat shield** wasn't damaged in the explosion.
The computer is up. Preparing to separate from the lander.

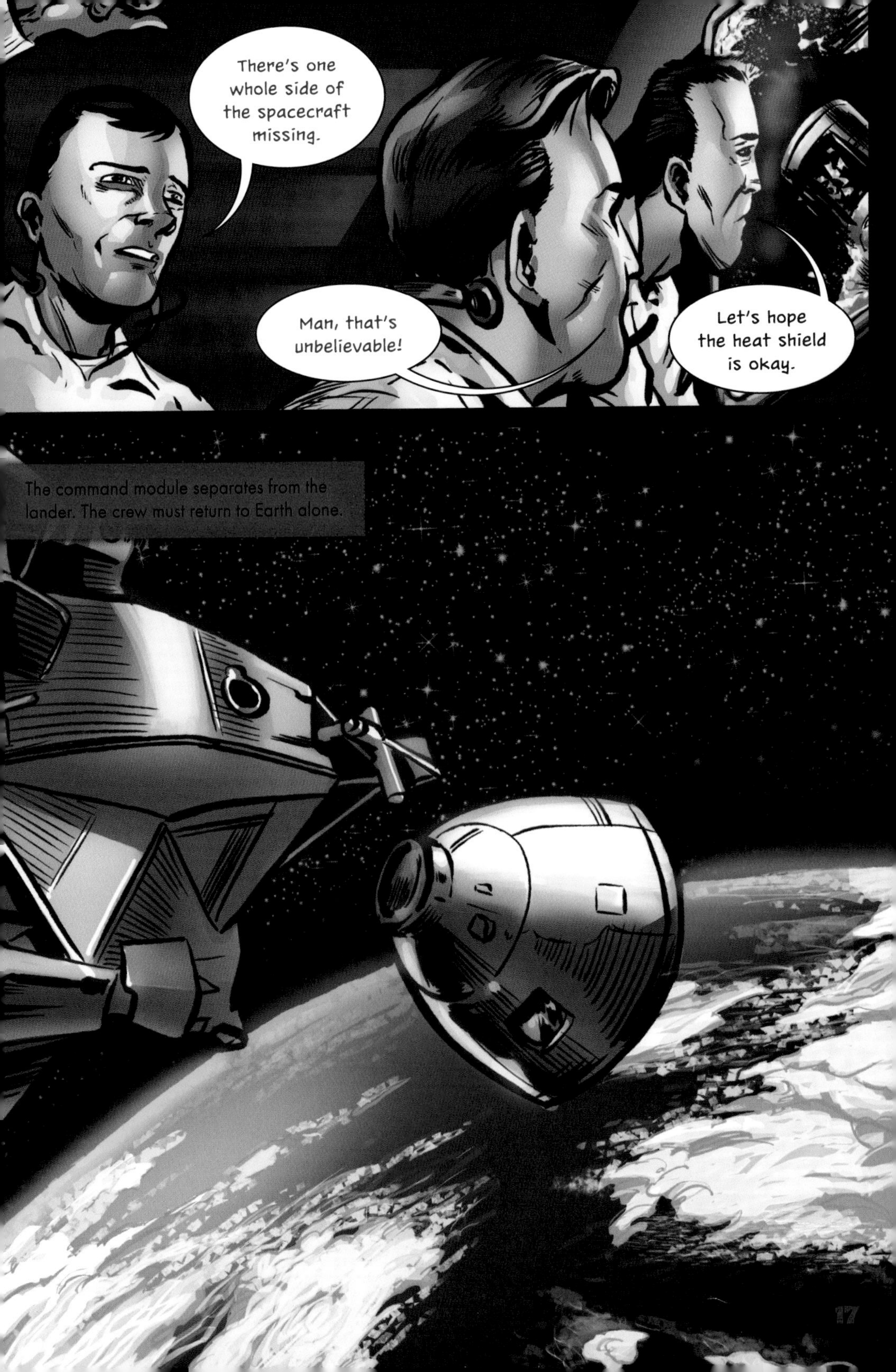
There's one whole side of the spacecraft missing.
Man, that's unbelievable!
Let's hope the heat shield is okay.
The command module separates from the lander. The crew must return to Earth alone.

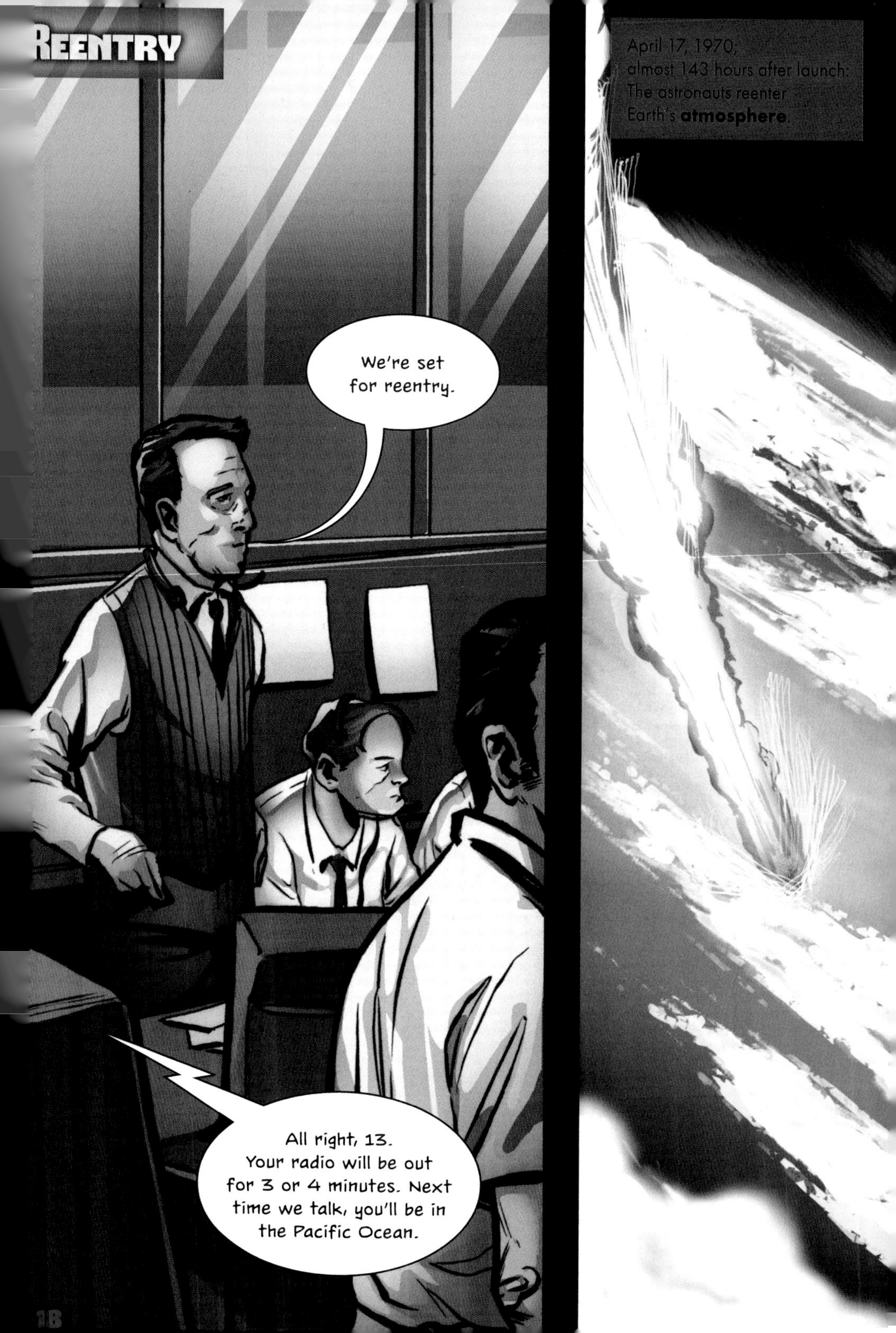
REENTRY
We're set for reentry.
All right, 13. Your radio will be out for 3 or 4 minutes. Next time we talk, you'll be in the Pacific Ocean.
April 17, 1970; almost 143 hours after launch: The astronauts reenter Earth's **atmosphere**.

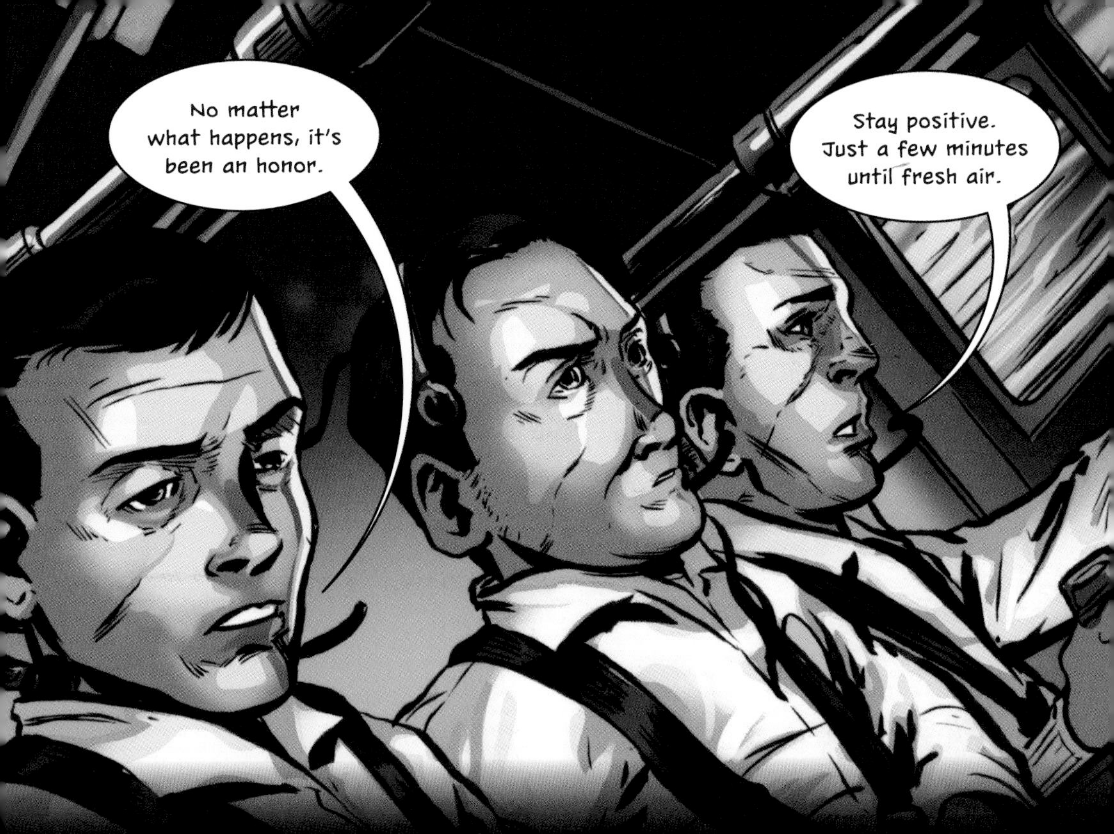
No matter what happens, it's been an honor.
Stay positive. Just a few minutes until fresh air.
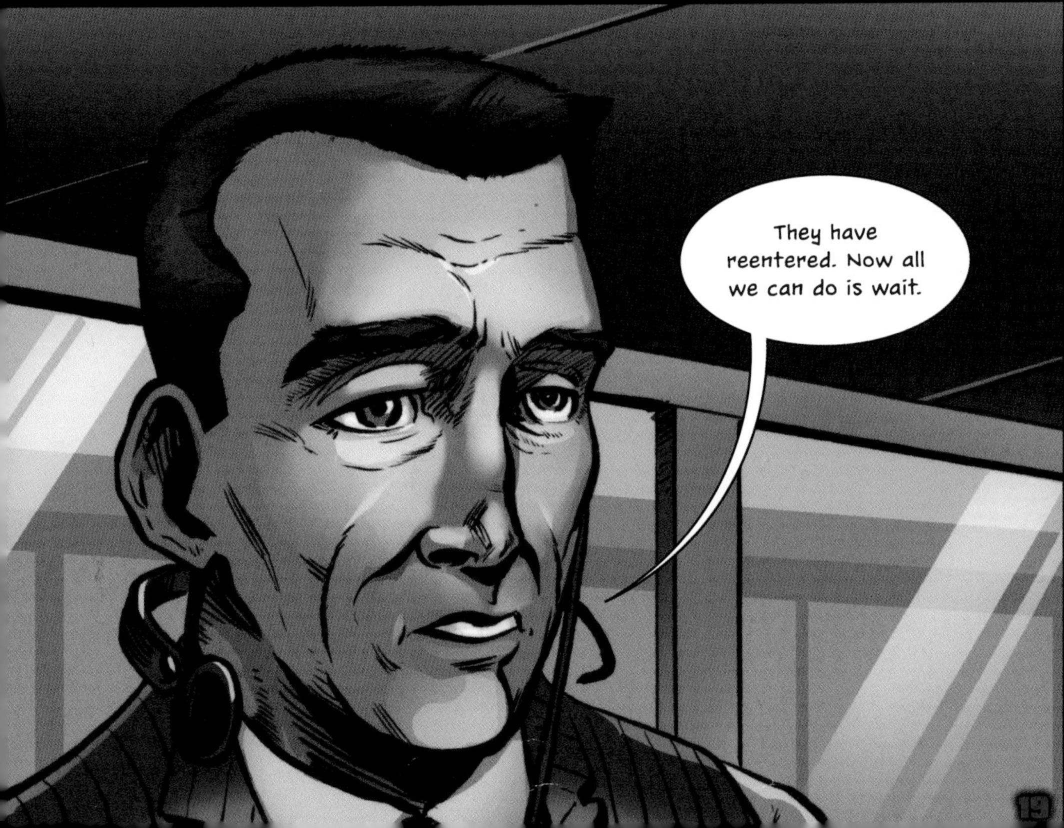
They have reentered. Now all we can do is wait.

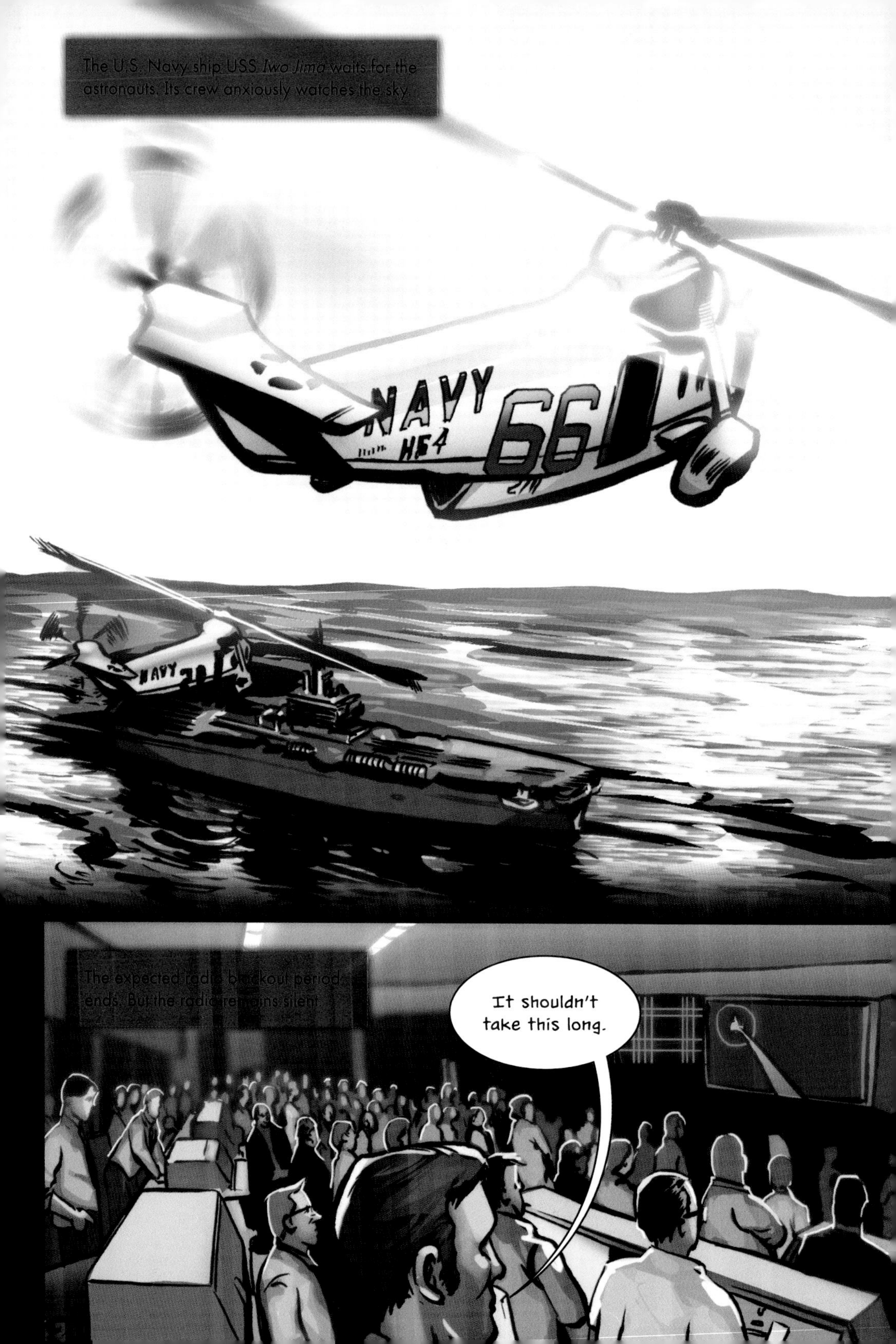

The U.S. Navy ship USS *Iwo Jima* waits for the astronauts. Its crew anxiously watches the sky.
NAVY 66 HS-4
NAVY
The expected radio blackout period ends. But the radio remains silent.
It shouldn't take this long.

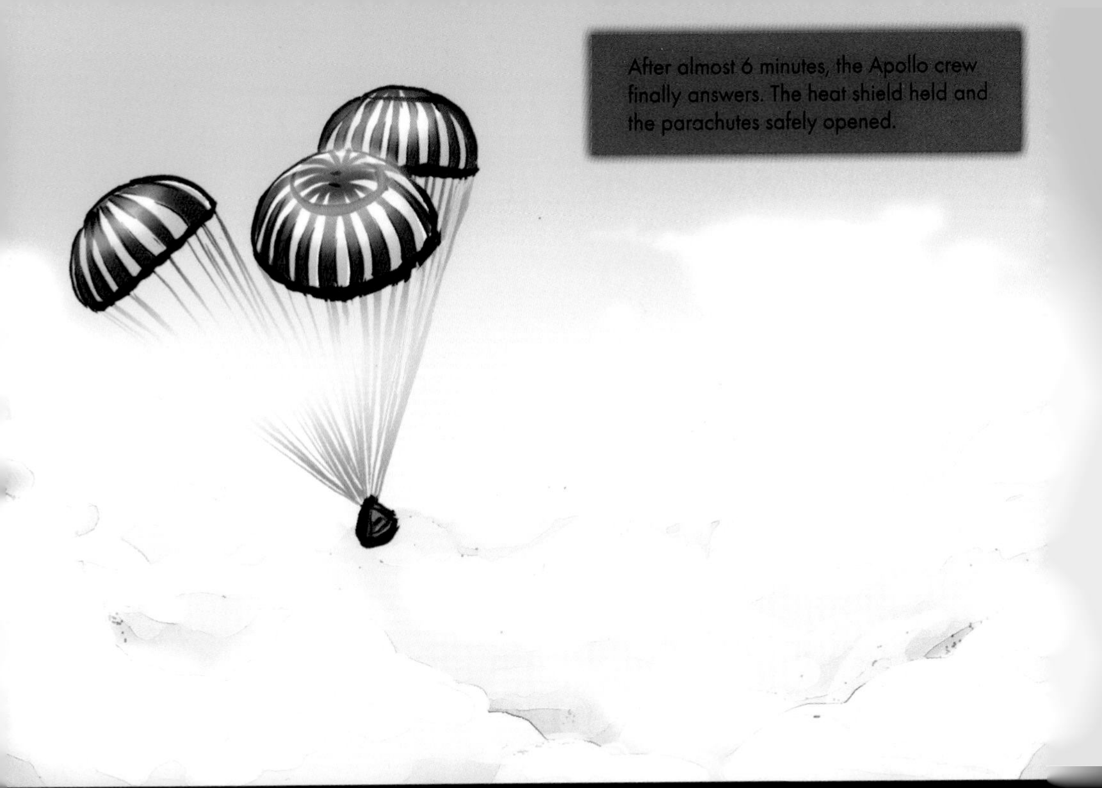
After almost 6 minutes, the Apollo crew finally answers. The heat shield held and the parachutes safely opened.

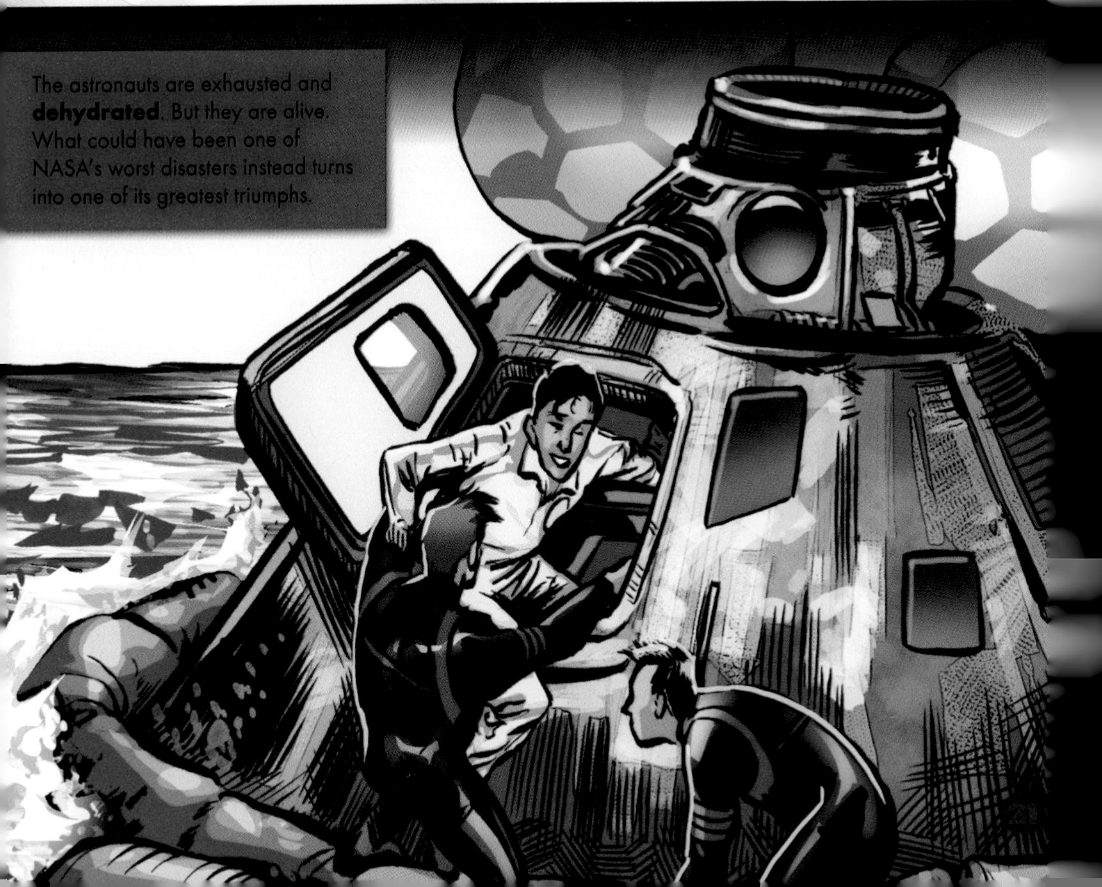
The astronauts are exhausted and **dehydrated**. But they are alive. What could have been one of NASA's worst disasters instead turns into one of its greatest triumphs.

MORE ABOUT THE DISASTER

- NASA calls the **Apollo** 13 **mission** a "successful failure" because the astronauts **made** it home safely.

- The Apollo 13 mission meant to land on the Fra Mauro area of the moon. About ten months later, the Apollo 14 mission successfully landed in that area to complete the research.

- At the time of the launch, Lovell was the world's most-traveled astronaut. He had spent a total of 572 hours, or almost 24 days, in space.

- Duct tape was a life-saving tool for the crew. With it, they created a device to limit the carbon dioxide in the cabin.

- The crew of Apollo 13 holds the world record for being the humans to travel the farthest distance from Earth.

Glossary

atmosphere—the blanket of air that surrounds Earth

burn—the controlled firing of a spacecraft's rocket engine

command module—the part of an Apollo spacecraft that served as the control center for the spacecraft

dehydrated—lacking enough water in the body

docks—connects to another spacecraft or space station

heat shield—the part of a spacecraft that deflects the heat generated by the spacecraft reentering Earth's atmosphere

lunar—related to the moon

lunar module—the part of an Apollo spacecraft that landed on the moon's surface; the lunar module was also called the lunar lander.

Mission Control—the command center for a space mission

NASA—short for the National Aeronautics and Space Administration; NASA is the agency that oversees U.S. space exploration.

reentry—the act of bringing a spacecraft back into Earth's atmosphere

service module—the part of an Apollo spacecraft that carried supplies and equipment for the mission

short circuit—an electrical failure in which electrical current is accidentally turned away from its intended route

To Learn More

AT THE LIBRARY

Bodden, Valerie. *To the Moon*. Mankato, Minn.: Creative Education, 2011.

Stone, Adam. *The Challenger Explosion*. Minneapolis, Minn.: Bellwether Media, 2015.

Waxman, Laura Hamilton. *Exploring Space Travel*. Minneapolis, Minn.: Lerner Publications Company, 2011.

ON THE WEB

Learning more about the Apollo 13 mission is as easy as 1, 2, 3.

1. Go to www.factsurfer.com.
2. Enter "Apollo 13 mission" into the search box.
3. Click the "Surf" button and you will see a list of related web sites.

With factsurfer.com, finding more information is just a click away.

Index